What's in a name?

Aaron

AIDAN

Aidan

Ali

Archie

Arnold

Arthur

AXE⌃

Axel

BAILLY

Min

Benjamin

Bill

Bob

Bradley

Brandon

Brent

Brent

Brody

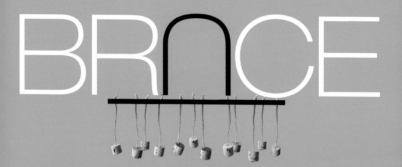

Bruce

Callum

Carl

Charlie

Christian

50%
OFF

Christopher

CcLl

Cliff

Clifford

damien

David

Name

Date of birth

0573/17

David

Dennis

Dennis

Dexter

Dominic

Drake

DUSTIN

Dustin

Edwin

Finn

Frank

Fred

Gabriel

Ge off

Geoff

GE or GE

George

Grayson

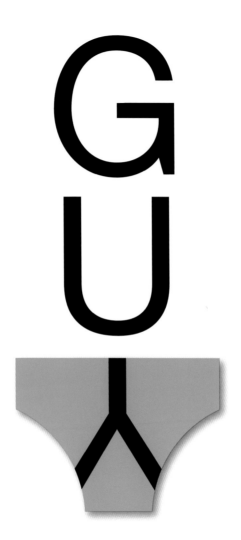

Guy

Harley

Harry

Harold

HAYDEN

Hayden

Hugh

Hugo

Jerry

JOHNNY

Junior

Justin NEW!

Kelvin

Larry

Lawrence

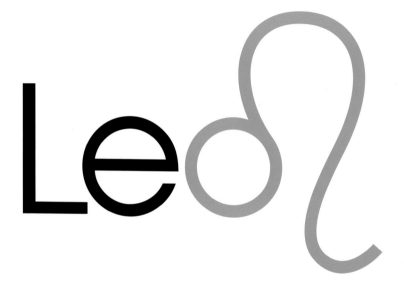

Leo

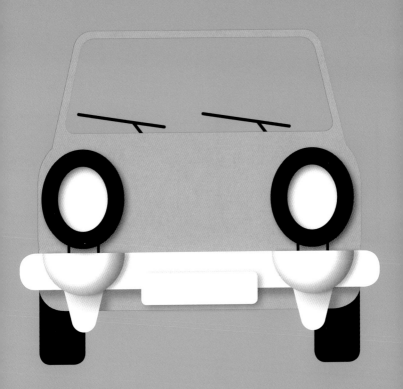

Luca

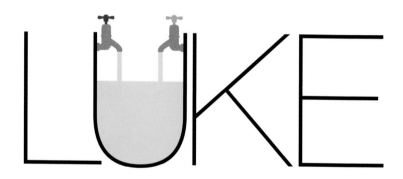

Luke

Mario

$\dfrac{8}{10}$ ⭐

Mark

arshall

Marshall

Matt

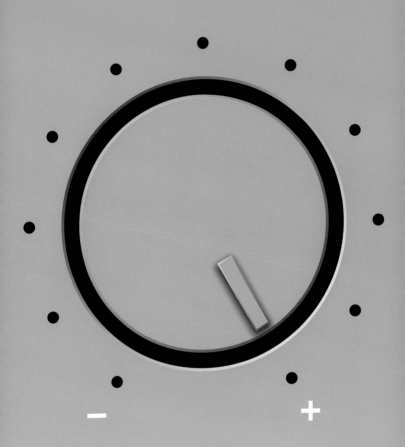

− +

Max

Mike

Morgan

Nelson

Nelson

Nick

Noah

Norman

OMEN

Owen

Pa

Patrick

Pete®

Peter

pH1

Pierce

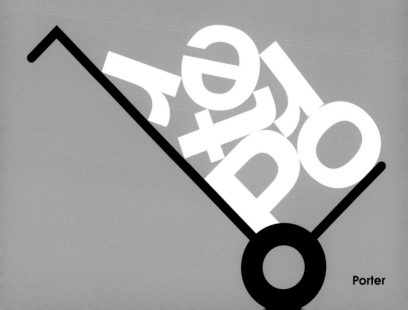

Porter

Preston

Ray

R391 N4LD

R$CHARD

RRT

Robert

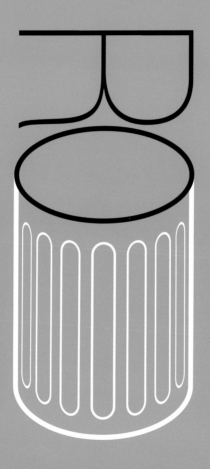

Robin

Rome ●

Romeo

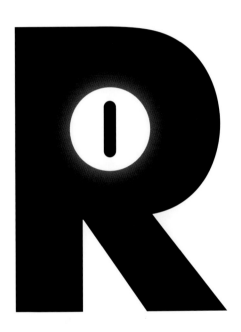

Ron

Sco

Scott

Spencer

STANLEY

Stuart

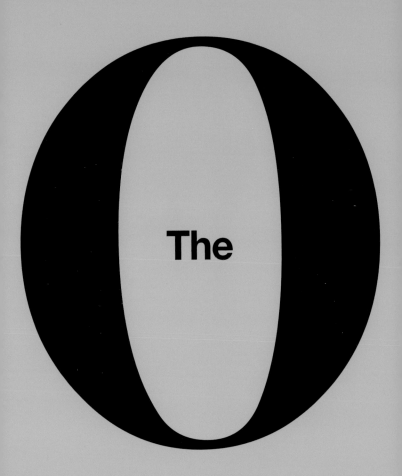

The

Theo

Toad

Todd

Torn

Tom

Tyre

Tyrell

Victor

Vin ent

Vincent

Will

Other titles by PatrickGeorge:

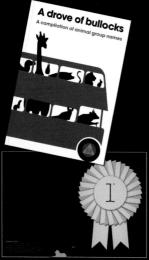

A pride of lions

A loveliness of ladybirds

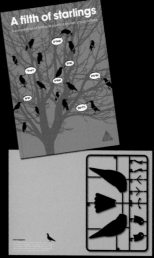

A kit of pigeons

A murder of crows

An implausibility of gnus

A huddle of penguins

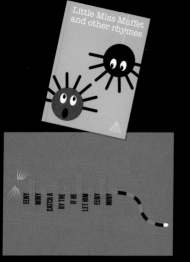

Little Miss Muffet and other rhymes

EENY MINY CATCH A BY THE IF HE LET HIM EENY MINY

The Grizzly Bear
is huge and wild,
He has devoured
the infant child,
The infant child
is not aware
He has been eaten
by the bear

One, two, three, four, five.
Once I caught a fish alive.
Six, seven, eight, nine, ten,
Then I let it go again.
Why did you let it go?
Because it bit my finger so.
Which finger did it bite?
This little finger on my right.

A dimple on your cheek,
you are gentle and meek.

A dimple on your chin,
you've a devil within.

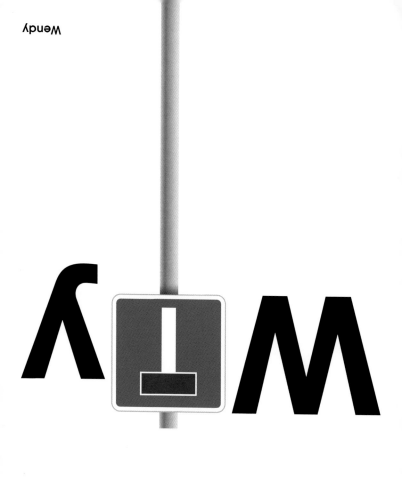

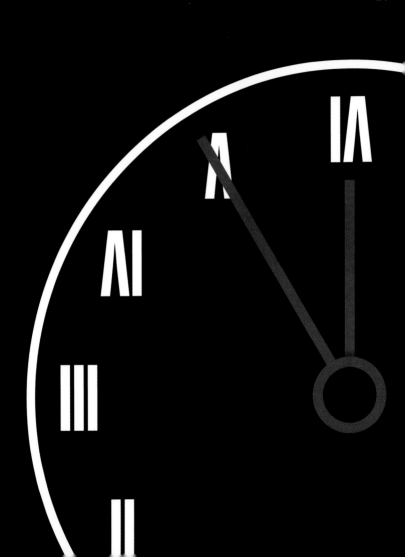

Victoria

Tracy

Tracy

Tonya

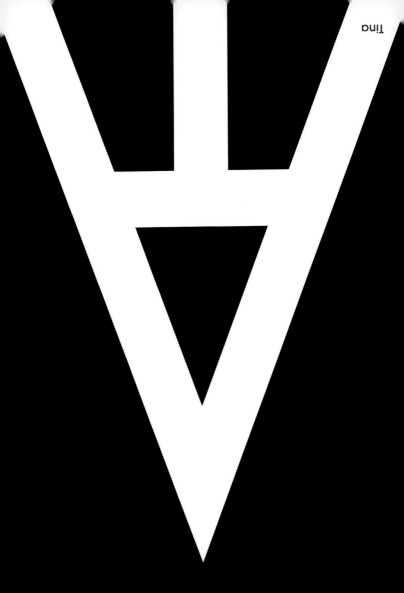

Thelma

Sylvia

sylvia

SUSAN

s+u+mmer

sophie

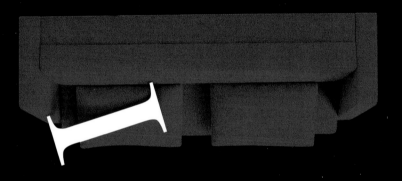

hell

y

S

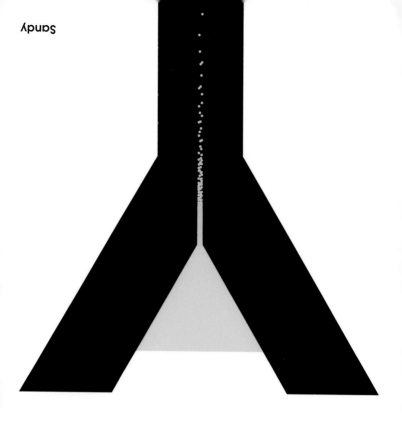

Sandy

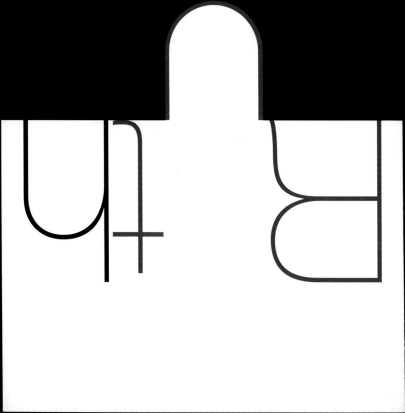

Rose

Pla ~~nce~~

PARENTAL ADVISORY
EXPLICIT CONTENT

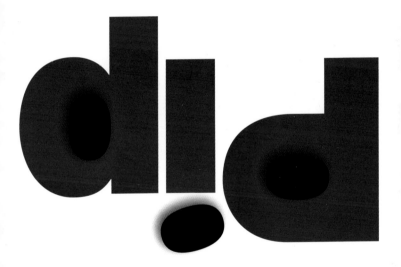

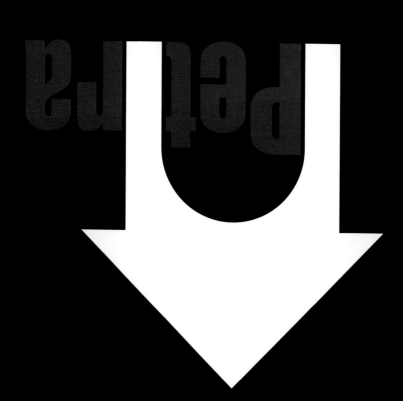

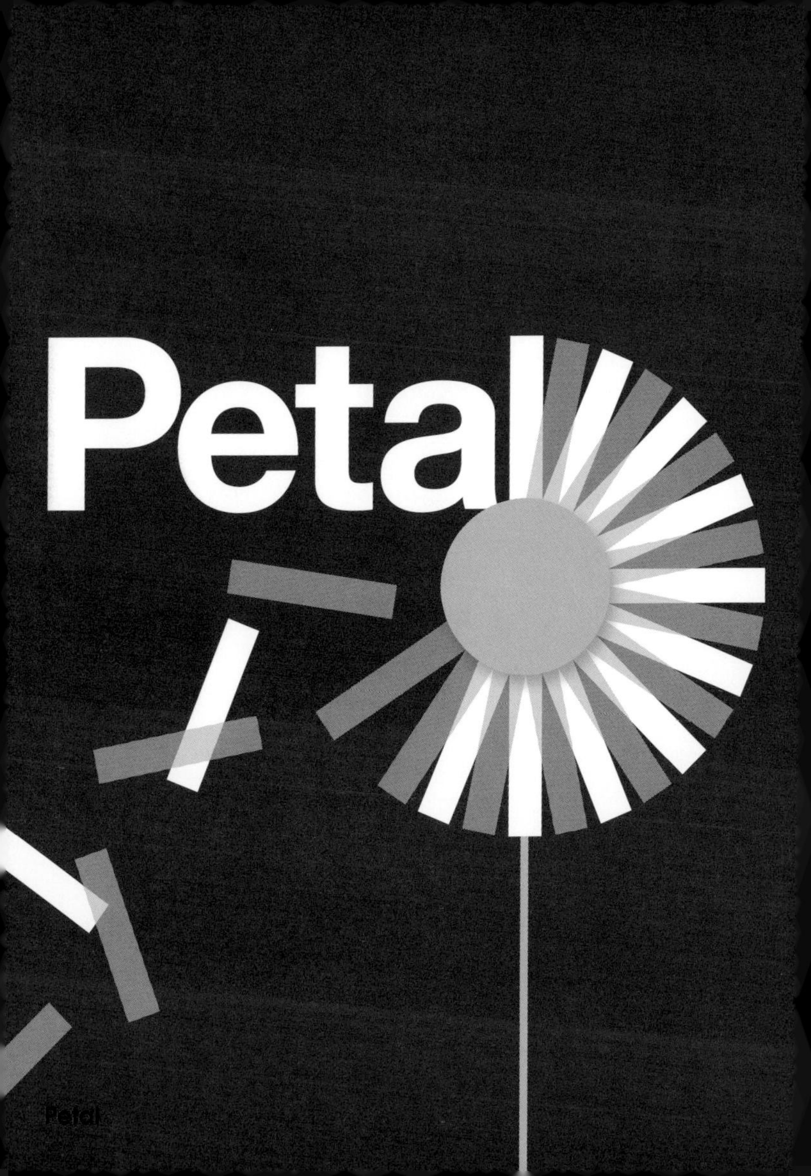
Petal
Petal

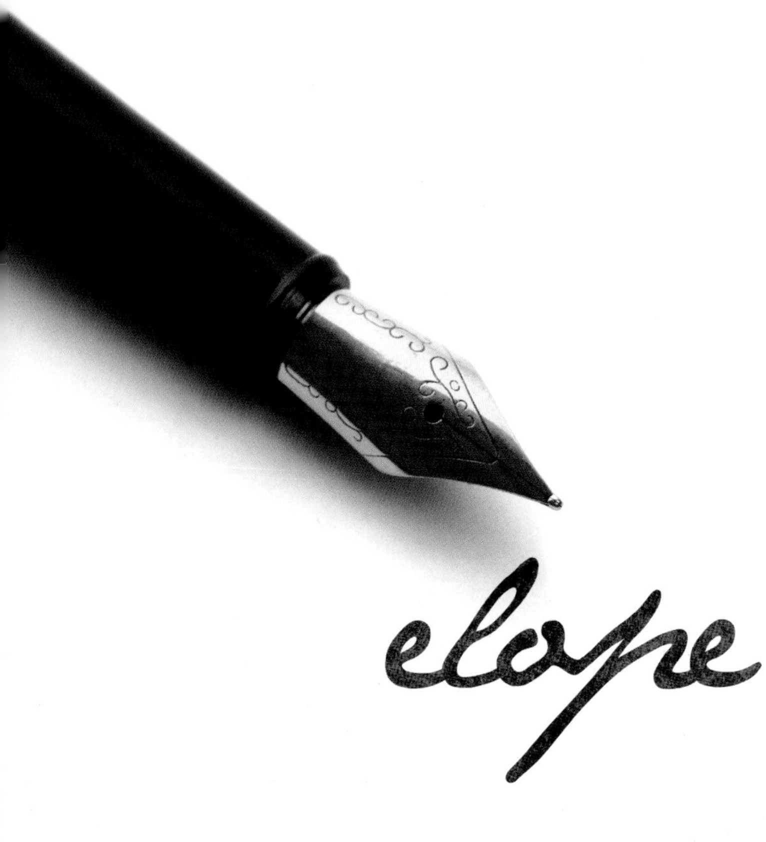

Penelope

Peggy

Olive

NATASHA

MARGARITA

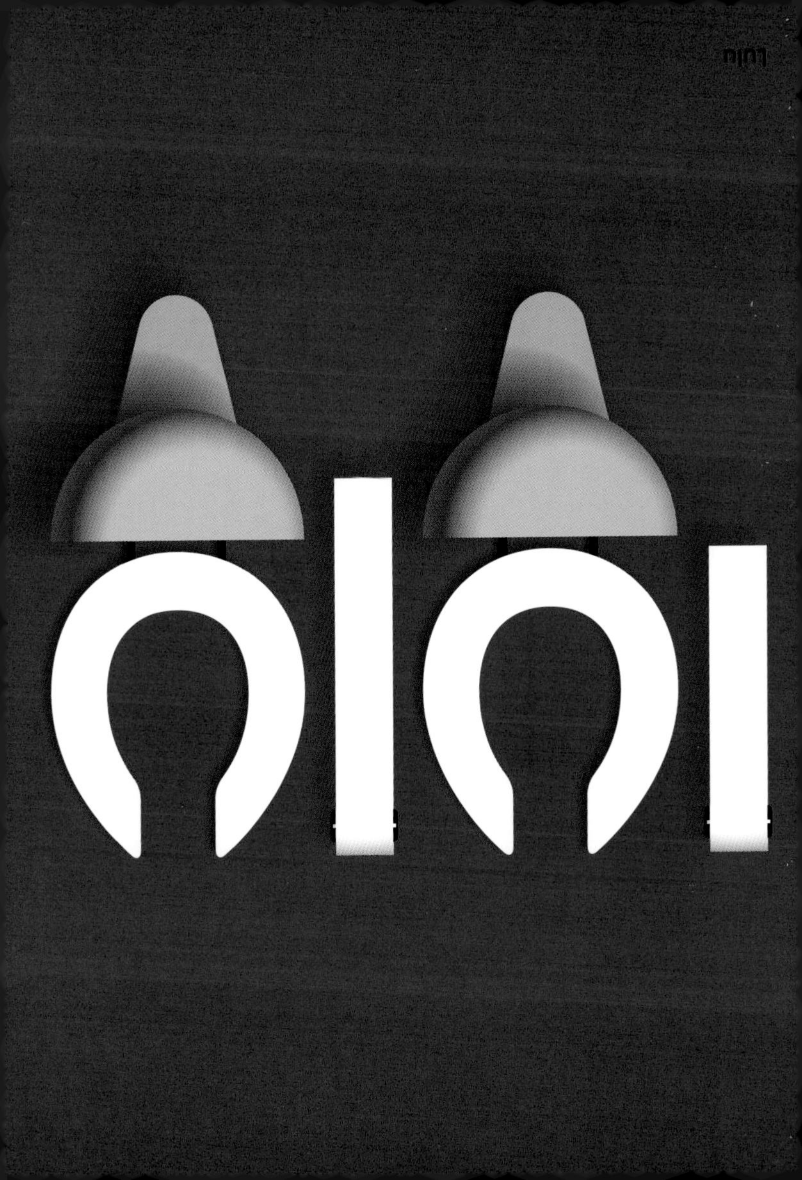

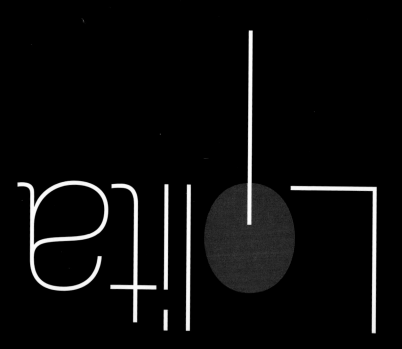

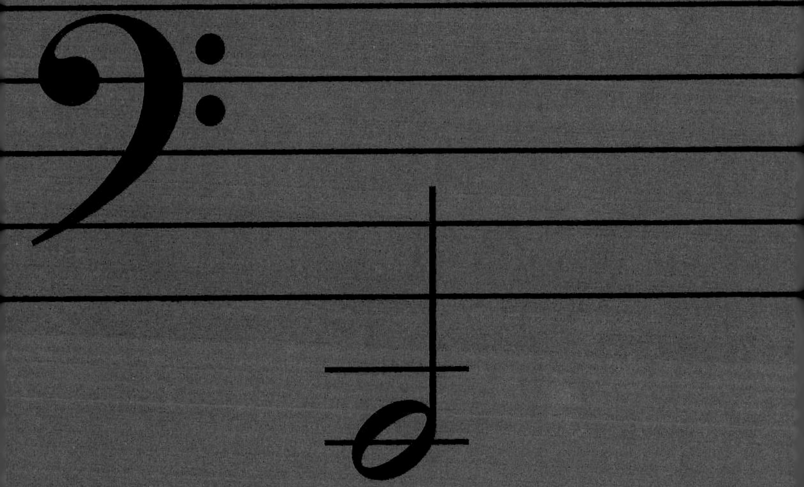

La

Leanda

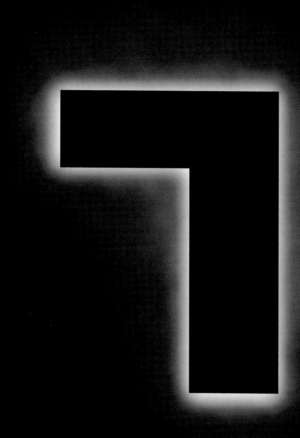

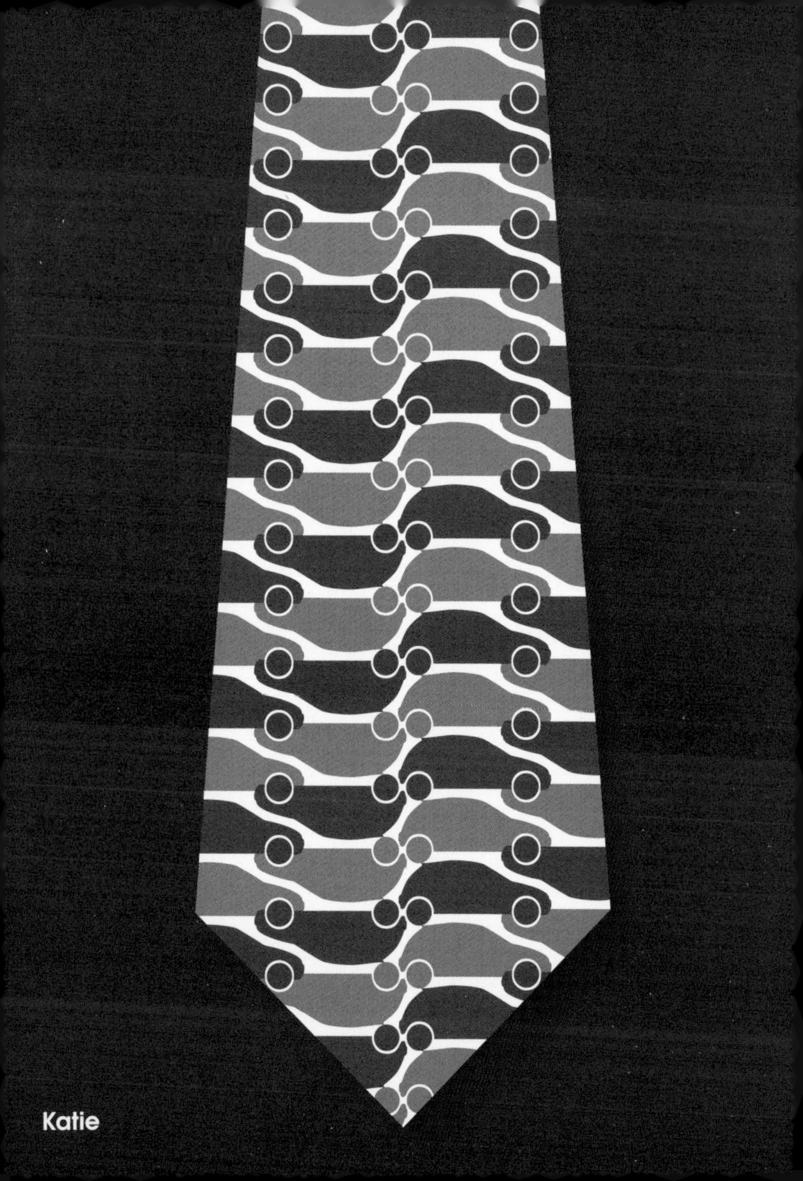
Katie

ine

Juliet

Joy :o)

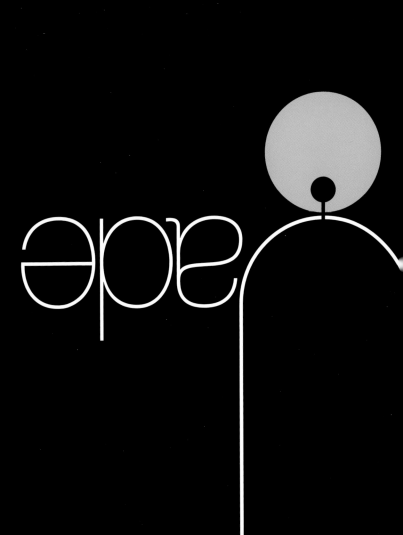

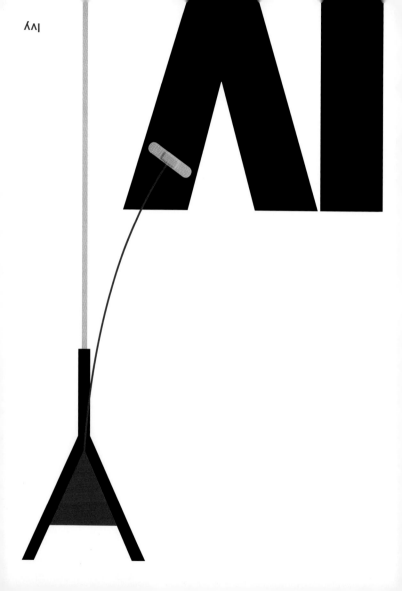

Ivy

INGRID

Heidi

Heidi

Hannah

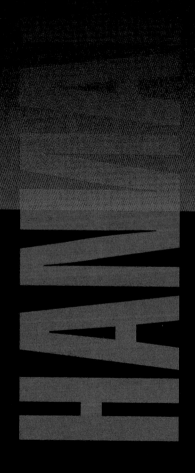

Faith

Faith

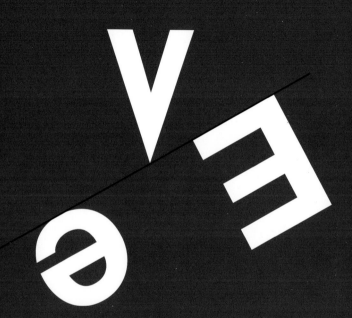

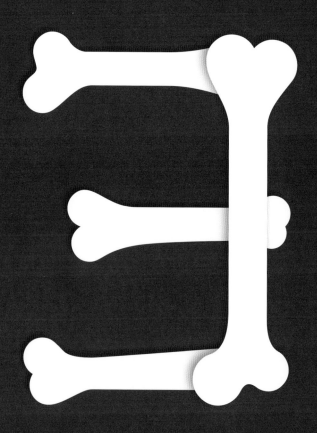

DINA

Nami!

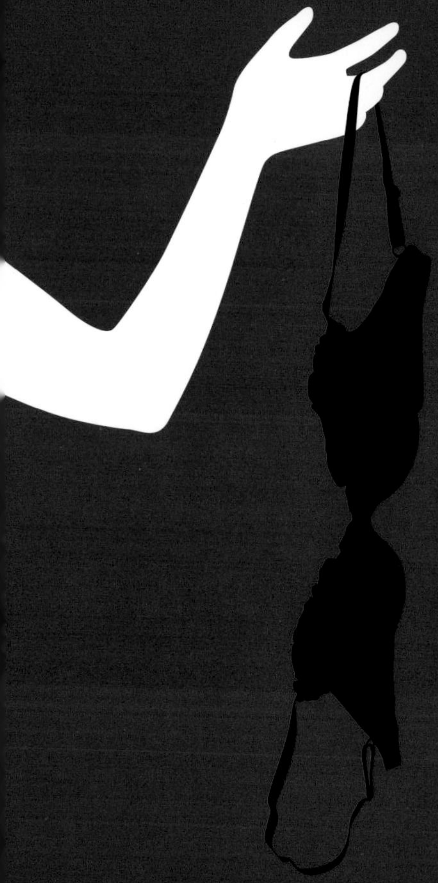

Debra

dawn

daisy

daisy

daisy

daisy

daisy

Courtney

COUR NEY

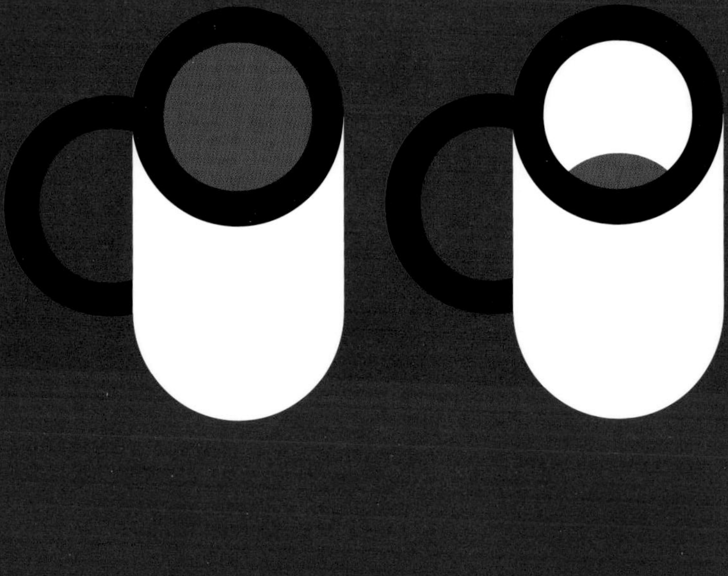

Coco

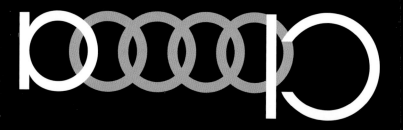

charity

Carrie

Caitlin

2in

3in

4in

5in

6in

Brooke

Billie

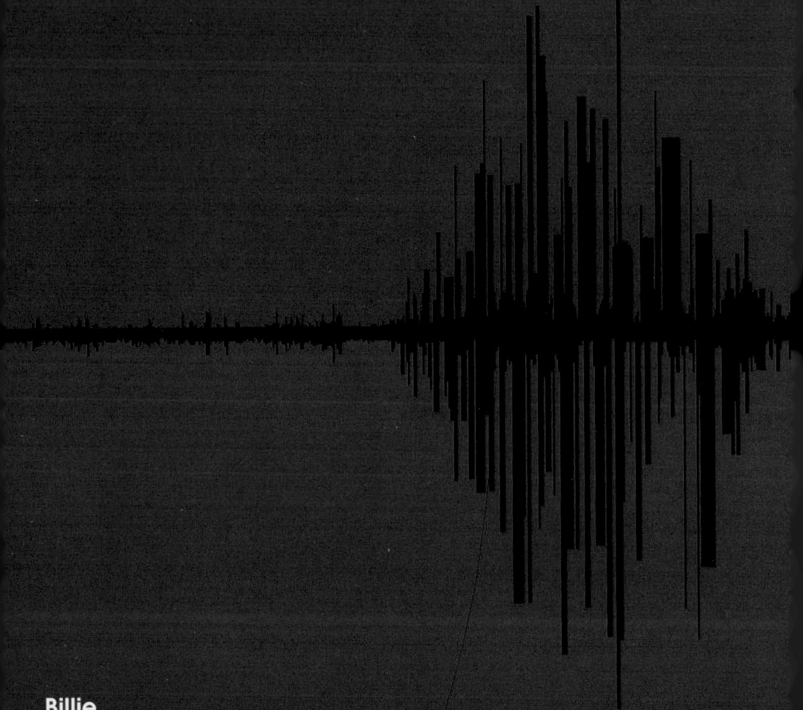

Billie

Betty

Bella

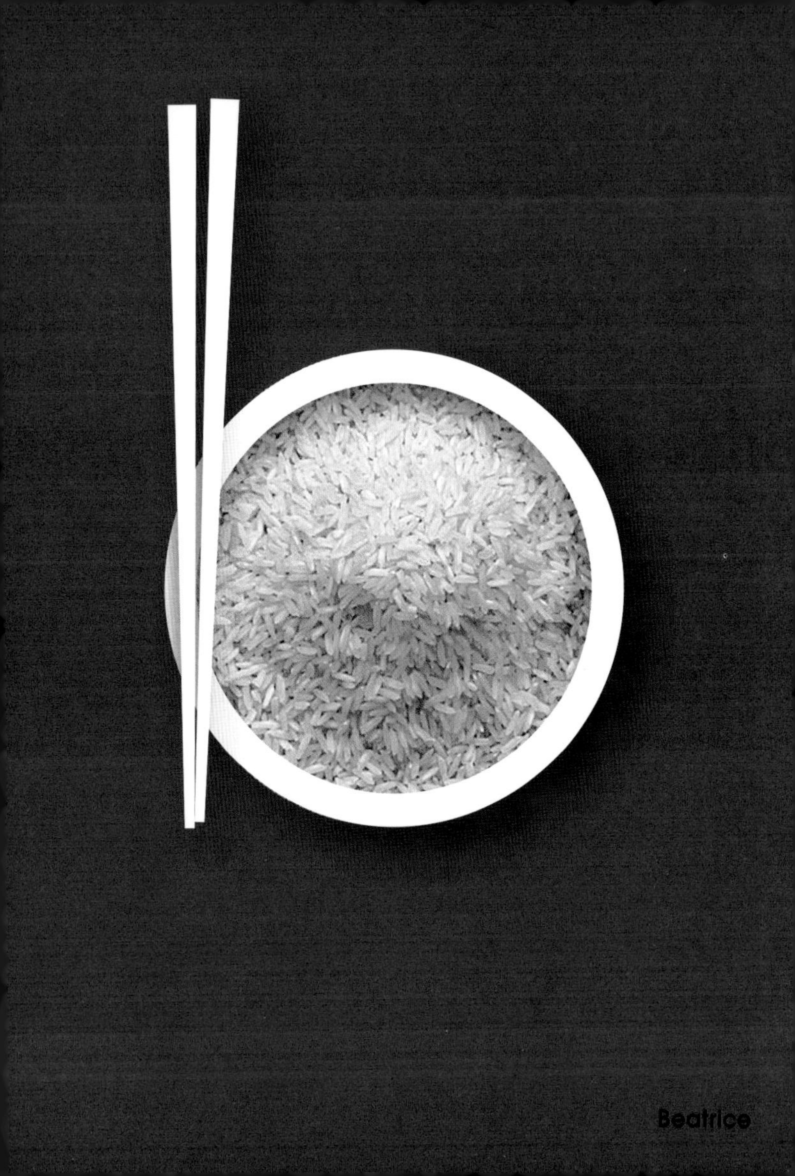
Beatrice

Astrid

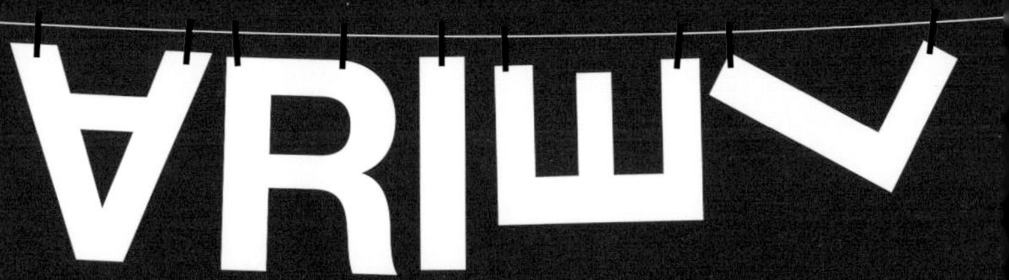

Ariel

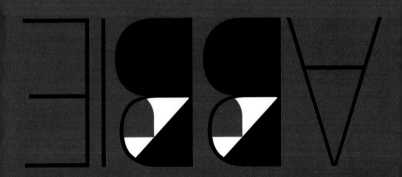

What's in a name?

For Laura

Copyright © PatrickGeorge 2010

Published in 2010 by
PatrickGeorge
46 Vale Square
Ramsgate
Kent CT11 9DA

ISBN 978-0-9562558-3-9

British Library Cataloguing in Publication Data.
A catalogue record for this book is available from the British Library.

Illustrated and designed by PatrickGeorge.
www.patrickgeorge.biz

Printed in England by Willow Print Services on Galerie Silk 150 gsm.
Galerie Silk is a PEFC certified paper.

Acknowledgements

Images appearing on *Amber*, *Barbara* and *Penelope* are used
under license from Shutterstock.com